ANIMALS IN DANGER

GALLERY BOOKS
An Imprint of W. H. Smith Publishers Inc.
112 Madison Avenue
New York City 10016

This edition first published in U.S.
in 1990 by Gallery Books,
an imprint of W.H. Smith Publishers, Inc.
112 Madison Avenue, New York, New York 10016

ISBN 0-8317-9586-7

Printed and bound in Spain

For rights information about the photographs in
this book please contact:

The Image Bank
111 Fifth Avenue, New York, N.Y. 10003

Producer: Solomon M. Skolnick
Author: Marcus Schneck
Design Concept: Leslie Ehlers
Designer: Ann-Louise Lipman
Editor: Madelyn Larsen
Production: Valerie Zars
Photo Researcher: Edward Douglas
Assistant Photo Researcher: Robert Hale

Title page: **Because of their luxurious fur and their scarcity, snow leopards are prime candidates for the illegal fur trade.** *Opposite:* **Elephant tusk ivory commands a price of more than $100 per pound. Perhaps as many as 300 African elephants are killed by poachers every day to supply the demands of illegal trade.**

Opposite: Family groupings and loyalties make elephants an easy mark for poachers with automatic rifles. Entire herds have been slaughtered for their ivory, their carcasses are left to rot. *This page:* A bull elephant emerges from a watering hole. The largest tusks ever recorded were those of the "Kilimanjaro Elephant," which weighed 460 pounds and were 24 feet around their curves when laid end to end.

The white rhino of Africa remains the most abundant of Earth's remaining rhinoceros, if a total population of about 4,600 can be described as abundant. Once numbering in the thousands, the northern herd has been reduced to about 20 animals. *Below:* Every part of these greater one-horned rhinoceros can be sold in the illegal animal trade, even the animal's urine, which is used in Asian folk remedies. *Opposite:* The horn of this black rhino could command a price of as much as $25,000 on the illegal market.

Cheetahs, the fastest land animals, can attain speeds of 40 miles per hour in pursuing prey. Their speed cannot help them escape man, however, who hunts them for their fur and because they attack livestock. *Opposite:* The tiger is one of the few animals that regularly preys on man. Its reputation made it a prized trophy for sport hunters as well. Consequently, it has been severely persecuted and today is extinct in most of its former range.

Everywhere on earth, animals are in danger. Not only are individual animals threatened by the hunter's bullet, the developer's bulldozer or the farmer's plow, but also entire populations, entire ecosystems, entire species are on the edge of extinction.

The reasons are many: ill-conceived and ill-fated agricultural practices in developing nations, development in delicate ecosystems, outright slaughter of entire herds of animals, to name but a few.

Man is simply too successful at producing more of himself than he can support. Consequently, ever-increasing portions of existing resources are consumed at an ever-increasing rate.

Among the means of destruction, poaching for the illegal, $1.5 billion-per-year trade in animals and animal parts may be the most insidious and hateful.

This page: **Tigers are strong swimmers and not at all hesitant to enter water, which can cover much of their extremely large home range. The primary threat to the species today is loss of habitat and fragmentation of what habitat remains. Lions once roamed over much of the globe. They survived in southeastern Europe as recently as 2,000 years ago. Today their numbers are dwindling and they are becoming rare outside of protected reserves, such as India's Forest of Gir, the only place that the Asian subspecies survives.** *Opposite:* **"King of Beasts" may never have been an accurate title for the lion, particularly the male, which lets the females do most of the hunting.**

Elephants and rhinoceros have been particularly vulnerable. In the last ten years, poachers have reduced the world's elephant population from 1.3 million to less than 400,000. For rhinos the numbers are even worse. The one-horned Java rhino now numbers 55 on Java and maybe another 10 to 15 in Vietnam, where it had been thought extirpated by war. The woolly Sumatran rhino is down to about 700.

The greater one-horned rhino, which once roamed all of southern Asia's floodplains, is confined to 1,200 to 1,500 animals in the most remote jungles of Nepal and India.

The most famous rhinos, those that became a symbol of wild Africa, now number only about 4,600 white and fewer than 3,800 black. While the southern subspecies of the white rhino has seen recent increases to the present 4,600, the northern population – numbering in the thousands in 1970 – has been reduced to just 22 animals.

A recent scientific discovery offers some hope for saving the black rhino. Because different subspecies of the animal are so genetically similar, they can be interbred. Thus conservationists can combine isolated populations of the animals into protected areas to increase breeding rates.

At the present time several African nations have efforts underway to protect rhinos, but often with disappointing results. Zimbabwe, for example, spends about a third of its parks budget in its war on poachers. Well-armed helicopter gunships and shoot-on-sight orders – part of "Operation Stronghold" – have been in progress, yet more than half of the 700 black rhinos in the nation's Zambezi River Valley were gunned down.

In a final attempt to save the remaining rhinos, the government has captured and moved more than 200 of them to protected areas, where they are under constant guard. Even so, the slaughter continues. Poachers, many armed with automatic assault rifles, are thought to kill 200 to 300 elephants per day. In Kenya they have reduced the population from 150,000 to fewer than 20,000.

The lure of fast, big money in nations with unbelievably low annual-per-capita incomes is simply too strong for some to ignore. Elephant tusk ivory sells for more than $100 per pound. A single rhino horn is worth up to $25,000 in the Far East, where it is used in making a folk remedy, or in the Middle East, where it is worked into a handle for a dagger.

The wild cats of the world have been decimated by the same, once-legal trade. Several hundred thousand furs of the ocelot alone were sold each year during the 1960s and 1970s. And, as recently as the mid-1980s, furs from the extremely endangered snow leopard were still being sold in India.

Opposite: **In some areas of central and east Africa leopards remain locally abundant, but the highly adaptable cat has become extinct in much of its former range, which included all of Africa as well as the Near and Middle East and several islands.**

The snow leopard developed from the same original animals as the lowland leopard, but developed a thicker and paler coat to contend with the specialized mountain environment of 8,500 to 19,700 feet above sea level in Tibet, Siberia and Afghanistan. *Below:* As man moved his cattle farther and farther into the jaguar's range, which once included the southern United States, persecution of the cat increased. Today it is locally extinct and endangered throughout its range.

Sport hunting, which continues for many of the cats, has also taken a heavy toll. But today's primary threats to the cats are loss of habitat to man and persecution for raids on livestock.

The lion, once one of the most widespread mammals with a nearly worldwide range, is becoming rare outside protected parks and reserves in Africa. The Asiatic subspecies survives only in India's Forest of Gir, where it is artificially managed.

The tiger, the largest cat and one of the few species that regularly preys on man, has a tenuous existence at best outside of protected areas. The jaguar, which once extended its range as far north as the southern United States, is in decline throughout Central and South America and locally extinct in many areas.

One of the most endangered cats, the Florida panther, has been reduced to just 20 to 50 animals, hemmed in by nonstop human population growth. A highway across the Everglades, known as Alligator Alley, is the major threat to the species' survival.

This page: **The traffic on Route 84 (Alligator Alley) through the Everglades is the most immediate threat to the Florida panther. A maximum of 50 Florida panthers, the last eastern subspecies of the American mountain lion, survive in tiny pockets of habitat in southern and central Florida.** *Opposite:* **The jaguar relies on ambush to take most of its prey, which can include everything from deer and domestic cattle to tapirs and monkeys.**

Since 1972, 18 cats have been killed or injured crossing the roadway. At the present time it is being lined with 10-foot-high fences along its entire length and equipped with about three dozen underpasses and bridges to supply "panther crossings."

Opposite: **Despite intense research and protection efforts, the Florida panther faces a clouded future.** *This page:* **In addition to habitat loss, the ocelot has been hunted ruthlessly for its valuable fur.** *Right:* **Destruction of the rainforest home of the jaguarundi is the greatest threat to the small, weasel-like cat, which is only 30 inches long and weights no more than 20 pounds.**

Human encroachment of a more violent and direct nature accounts for the devastation that has come to two other groups of animals as man has spread farther across the globe. With few exceptions, whenever wolves or bears come into contact with man, they are much worse off for the encounter.

In response to, and often in anticipation of, real or perceived threats to himself or his livestock, man has waged war on these animals. Traps, poisons, heavy arms, aircraft and even biological warfare have been employed, and still are whenever conflict arises in those few places that the animals have managed to persist.

Combined with a once-booming fur trade, particularly in wolf pelts, man has had his "desired" impact. Enough gray wolves survive in a few last strongholds, such as Alaska and parts of Canada, that governments still allow hunting and trapping for them. However, there are only a few small populations anywhere south of the Canadian border, and these are strictly protected.

One subspecies of the gray wolf – the Mexican wolf – survives only as a captive group of 30 animals. Likewise, the only red wolves alive today are third and fourth generations of captive animals, and some of those are suspected crossbreeds with part-coyote ancestry. Limited reintroduction efforts may someday see truly wild packs of the canines living and hunting in extremely protected and isolated reserves.

The brown or grizzly bear, the largest living carnivore on Earth, has met a similar fate. The animal remains locally abundant in the Soviet Union, where nearly two-thirds of the estimated world population of 100,000 exists. But only a remnant population of perhaps 1,000 survives in the American west, apart from Alaska.

Not even primates – man's closest relatives – have escaped devastation. The chimpanzee, one of the few animals to use tools, has been captured and exported from Africa in large numbers for zoos, biomedical research and the pet trade. As recently as the early 1980s, a few were still being exported. The conventional means of capture involves killing mothers, and often the others in bands of up to 80 chimps, to take the young.

Opposite: Alleged attacks on humans by healthy wolves are extremely exaggerated, as are many of the concerns of cattlemen over predation on their livestock. Nevertheless, strong opposition rises whenever a reintroduction of the species is contemplated. *This page:* Much of the natural range of the kit fox has been destroyed to make way for agricultural uses of the land. Also, the population was adversely affected by attempts to eradicate coyote and wolf populations through poisoning. The only purebred red wolves alive today are third-and fourth-generation offspring of a small captive pack of the animals. Man's ravages, as well as the interbreeding with the highly successful coyote, has brought the pure species to the edge of extinction. *Overleaf:* The hair-raising cry of the gray wolf can still be heard through much of Canada and Alaska and in a few isolated areas south of the Canadian border.

Gorillas, often killed for only their heads and hands, have stabilized and even increased their numbers in several protected areas of Africa. A particularly successful program in Rwanda allows tourists to visit the gorillas in the wild, providing a measure of protection through the presence of people and giving the animals some value in the eyes of local residents.

While the direct attack of man has been responsible for a shamefully long list of lost species, for many – including the chimpanzee and gorilla – habitat loss has been even more harmful.

The world's rainforests are the current target, as man continues his ever-widening conversion of natural environments for his own purposes.

This round of "development" probably will be the most devastating yet.

Although the 2 billion acres of remaining rainforests cover only 7 percent of Earth's land-mass, they are home to more than half of all animal and plant species.

These important environments are disappearing at the rate of 25 to 50 acres every minute. Their vegetation, where most of the nutrients in the rainforest system are stored, is being clear-cut or torched to make way for agricultural practices that the soil will be able to support for only a few years. Photographs taken in September 1988 from the U.S. Space Shuttle *Discovery* revealed a million-square-mile cloud of smoke over South America's Amazon River Basin.

As the inappropriate farmland advances, species that haven't even been recorded yet are being lost forever. "Without firing a shot, we may kill one-fifth of all species of life on this planet within the next twenty years," according to the World Wildlife Fund.

Opposite: **Two brown bears dispute fishing rights to a section of salmon-rich river. Confrontations are common when the big bears congregate around prime locations along the rivers.** *This page:* **Perhaps 100,000 brown bears remain in the world today and most are in the Soviet Union. Whenever bear and man occupy the same territory, the bear generally is the loser. The brown bear is the largest living carnivore, but the hulking creature will generally avoid confrontation with man. Startled individuals and sows defending cubs are notable and dangerous exceptions. An animal that can weigh move than 1,000 pounds can consume a great deal of fish in one day.**

Another estimate warns that 17,500 animals and plants are being lost to extinction each year in these forests. The Office of Technological Assessment, the research arm of the U.S. Congress, points out that species are disappearing even faster than they did when the dinosaurs vanished 65 million years ago.

The island republic of Madagascar is among the world leaders in species loss due to such deforestation, combined with uncontrolled population growth and unregulated hunting. This is particularly disastrous because the Texas-size island, owing to its isolation by about 250 miles of ocean, has given rise to an incredible array of unique species.

The lemurs, a diverse group of tree-dwelling primates, are the most well-known of these strange creatures, but most of the island's other life is equally unique. For example, 233 of its 250 reptiles and eight of its nine carnivores are found nowhere else.

Already gone from the island, and consequently from the entire earth, are animals like the elephant bird, which laid eggs weighing 20 pounds each, and more than a dozen species of lemurs.

The giant panda, which is commonly and mistakenly thought to be a bear, has been in decline for centuries. Hunting by man, habitat loss and long-term climatic changes are the primary reasons. *Below:* Of the nearly 1,000 giant pandas that remained in the wild in the 1970s, many died as a result of a massive die-off of bamboo, the nearly exclusive diet item for the animal. *Opposite:* Although some giant pandas are kept in zoos, the species' breeding success in captivity has been dismal. Captive animals are not a self-sustaining population.

Although only 10 percent of Madagascar remains covered in native vegetation, the discovery of previously unknown species is almost routine. The golden-crowned sifaka, a lemur of which only a few hundred are thought to exist, was only recently determined to be a distinct species.

While most such species-wide destruction is occurring in developing countries, finger-pointing serves no purpose. The developed world has its own blood-stained history, one which seems to be the model for today's catastrophes.

Opposite: By 1950, there were only 30 of the diminutive key deer surviving on the islands in the lower Florida Keys. By the mid-1970s, the population had recovered to more than 400 animals. Logging of the mixed forest habitat of the woodland caribou (reindeer) is the primary threat to the species. In Finland, where the majority of the animals still exist, some old forest areas are being left for the caribou's use and reintroduction programs are bolstering the herds. *This page:* Most subspecies of the white-tailed deer are increasing their numbers enormously, but a few, like the Columbian white-tailed deer, are struggling. Hybridization with the Columbian black-tailed deer is today's greatest threat to the Columbian white-tailed deer, which inhabits a limited area along the lower Columbia River. The pampas deer of South America is protected throughout its range, although enforcement in many areas is lax. Uncontrolled hunting and habitat loss continue to decimate the population.

Mountain gorillas probably have never been very common. The existing population numbers about 400, with continued occasional kills by poachers. A tourist/ conservation program in Rwanda allows visitors to meet mountain gorillas on their own turf, providing a measure of protection for the animals. *Opposite:* The lowland gorilla is most numerous, with a population of about 20,000. Poachers often kill the magnificent beasts for the head and paws alone.

For example, in the few hundred years that Western man has been in North America, 70-plus species of animals that once flourished on the continent have become extinct. The Labrador duck of the northeast vanished so quickly that no one ever found and recorded its nesting grounds. The last passenger pigeon, a bird that some observers reported in flocks of millions in the early 1800s, died in 1914 in the Cincinnati Zoo.

The United States' national emblem, the bald eagle, came dangerously close to becoming extinct a few decades ago, victim of the pesticides that man has been pumping into the environment. After a significant recovery over the past fifteen years, recent counts have placed the bird at about 4,500 in the lower 48 states and 30,000 in Alaska.

Many other species, though, will never have that same opportunity. Of the 9,000 known species of birds on earth, more than 1,000 – about 11 percent – were in danger of extinction by 1988, according to the International Council for Bird Preservation. That number had jumped about 400 percent in 10 years.

Habitat loss is closing in on the orangutan, which is now confined to Borneo and Sumatra. The pet and zoo trade took their toll in the past. *Opposite:* Orangutans often find themselves overcrowded as their forest home is destroyed. Displaced individuals have become ill-tempered wanderers, impacting the social structures and breeding success of other groups.

Other, perhaps less obvious, results of man's activities will irrevocably affect the earth's remaining species.

The full impact of acid rain is yet to be seen, but research has given some fairly strong clues. The forests and rice paddies around China's most-populated and most-polluted cities are already extremely troubled by the manmade atmospheric condition. Down-wind from those forests and paddies is the Xishuangbanna Nature Reserve, home to the endangered Asian elephant, crested gibbon (an ape), forest guar (a wild cow) and others.

Civil unrest, endemic to many areas of the earth that also house the greatest diversity of wildlife, can be a recurring threat. The addax (an antelope adapted to desert life) and many other rare arid-region animals, such as 80 percent of the world's scimitar oryx, were protected in significant numbers for many years in Chad's Ouadi Rime-Ouadi Achim Faunal Reserve. Then, in 1978 when civil war broke out, the government abandoned the reserve.

One of the few animals to use tools, the chimpanzee is also one of species most impacted by animal trade. Large numbers were exported from Africa for biomedical research, zoos and the pet industry. The red uakari, shown here, and the white uakari are the only short-tailed primates in South America. Hunting for food is the main threat, although they are protected in much of their range. *Opposite:* Gelada baboons live in male-led troops, some-times congregating in groups of hundred. Agricultural demands on their range are a primary threat, but the males are also hunted for their capes.

About 1,000 of the once fairly common addax survive today in isolated pockets in the desert regions of Chad, Mauritania, Niger and Mali. They are under constant threat from hunters, drought, lack of food and harassment by photo-seeking tourists in vehicles.

Tourism may similarly be threatening the humpback whale, listed as endangered since 1966. Noise from jetskis, motorboats and the like in the whale's winter breeding grounds of Hawaii's coastal waters is forcing cows and their calves constantly farther from shore into less friendly waters.

The oceans are far from immune from the ravages of man, and their largest inhabitants appear to be among the most imperiled. Many may be even more endangered than previously thought.

Opposite: **A female lar (or common) gibbon tends to her infant. Gibbons make a wide variety of calls, including booms that can be heard over a couple of miles.** *This page:* **Extensive deforestation has fragmented Central and South America's populations of spider monkeys, which were previously hard-hit by the pet trade that exported thousands of them to the United States. A few hundred golden lion tamarins survive in a reserve in southeast Brazil. Unfortunately, the reserve is poorly protected from encroachment and depredations.**

Lemurs, such as this red ruffed, have come to fill an incredibly large number of ecological niches in the isolation of Madagascar and nearby islands. Relentless destruction of the island's natural environment is threatening many species that exist nowhere else. The hanuman langur is considered sacred in much of India, a fact that doesn't seem to provide any measure of protection from widespread habitat destruction. *Opposite:* The Vietnam War, with its unprecedented use of defoliants, took a heavy toll on the world's population of douc langurs. In addition, Vietnamese soldiers saw the small primate as a ready source of meat.

Kangaroos, like this forester kangaroo, are widely persecuted because they compete with livestock for habitat. They are also hunted for their skins. *Below:* Little is known about the status of Baird's tapir, except that the animal is declining throughout its Central American range. Habitat destruction and hunting for meat threatens all species of tapirs. *Opposite:* The slow-moving three-toed sloth is equally slow to adaptation, such as the widespread destruction of its rainforest home. The animal also does poorly in captivity.

About 300 American crocodiles exist today, long ago pushed from the historical nesting sites in the mangrove swamps that are now Miami Beach. The saltwater species clings on at the southern tip of Florida.

Top to bottom: Nile crocodiles, among the largest, can grow to more than 16 feet in length and weigh more than 2,000 pounds. They have been known to prey on man. Crocodiles, such as these in Cuba, are often seen as a threat and a pest by local residents, although research has shown that they make valuable contributions to their watery habitats. The Cuban crocodile is found only in the Zapata Swamp.

Annual summer surveys by the International Whaling Commission (IWC) since 1978 have found only 453 blue whales in their traditional feeding grounds off Antarctica, where scientists had expected to find about 4,500. Before commercial whaling, there were probably more than 200,000 blue whales. Even the sperm whale, the most abundant of the great whales today, has been so depleted by hunting that no kill quotas are set by the IWC. The greatest kill of these 55-ton creatures was about 30,000 between 1963 and 1964, but the harvest remained at more than 20,000 through the mid-1970s.

Other sea inhabitants, notably seals and sea otters, have met similar commercial fates, but with protection have started to rebound.

The American alligator recovered so well under protection— despite continued poaching—that it has been removed from the endangered species list and some southern states now have regulated hunting seasons. *Opposite:* As the American alligator recovered from near-extinction, complaints mounted over the large crocodilian's appearance in swimming pools, appetite for pets and even attacks on humans.

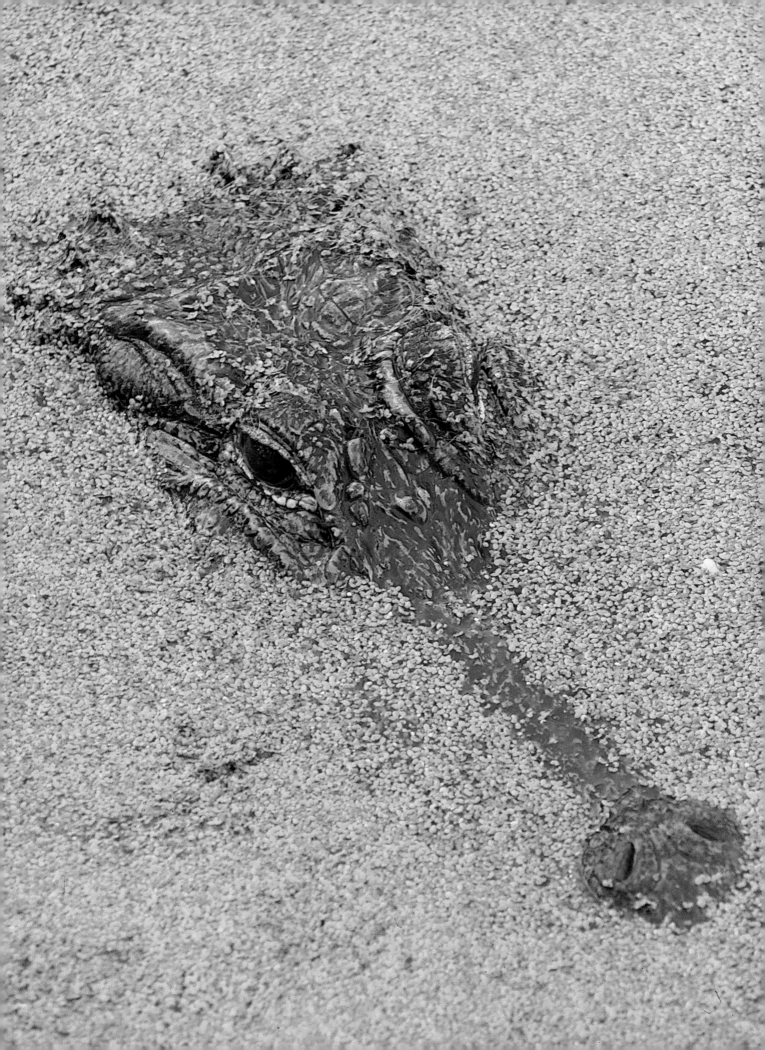

The Guadalupe fur seal, which numbered more than 200,000 before commercial hunting, was declared extinct in 1928. Then, in 1949, a lone bull was located, followed by a colony of 14 on Guadalupe Island off Baja California. Current estimates now place this seal population at more than 1,500.

The sea otter had been hunted so heavily for its valuable pelt by 1911 that only 1,000 to 2,000 remained. With protection and reintroductions, the population has slowly increased.

The Guadalupe fur seal and the sea otter represent the brighter side of a mostly dismal situation for endangered – and soon to be endangered – species. And they are not totally isolated success stories.

The American alligator, once endangered, has recovered to the point that it can be legally hunted. The oryx, the last wild herd of which was killed by hunters in 1972, saw the first new wild-birth of a calf in 1982 in a reintroduced herd in Oman.

Opposite: The land iguana of the Galápagos proved easy prey for man and his introduced species. *This page:* The Komodo dragon is the largest lizard on Earth today, growing to a length of 10 feet and a weight of 300 pounds. The reptile will prey on animals as large as deer and pugs. One estimate places the number of tortoises removed from the Galápagos islands by whaling ships for fresh meat at 10 million. Even after the whalers' demand for the giant tortoises passed, the feral dogs, cats and rats introduced to the islands continued to prey on all but the largest of the reptiles.

When the bald eagle was designated the national emblem of the United States in 1782, there were an estimated 90,000 of the birds in existence. *Opposite:* Pesticides such as DDT were pumped into the environment. Many populations of birds of prey, including the bald eagle, suffered as a consequence.

Recent counts have recorded a remarkable recovery in the bald eagle during the past 15 years. Numbers are estimated at 4,500 in the lower 48 states and 30,000 in Alaska. In the wake of the March 24, 1989, oil spill by the *Exxon Valdez* in Prince William Sound— where 360 nesting pairs normally nest— U.S. Fish & Wildlife Service personnel found only 46 active nests by the end of June 1989. By September 1989, a total of 146 dead eagles had been found. *Opposite:* The monkey-eating eagle, which was never found outside of the Philippines, is one of the world's rarest eagles. About 50 pairs remain.

Mauritius' pink pigeon, of which there were only 13 in the wild at one time, has increased to a population of more than 100 through a captive breeding program.

Organizations like World Wildlife Fund, International Union for the Conservation of Nature and Natural Resources, Greenpeace, and Gerald Durrell's Wildlife Preservation Trust International are pumping large amounts of money, personnel and effort into the fight to save those species that are still savable.

Many governments are arriving at a new understanding of the value and necessity of the natural heritage inside their manmade borders, as well as across the entire planet.

Opposite: Innocence of isolation made the Galápagos hawk easy prey for the first settlers to the islands, who clubbed thousands of them to death to protect their introduced poultry species. *Below:* More than 1,200 pairs of peregrine falcons have been recorded in the wild, more than four times the number counted in the 1970s. DDT-caused problems with eggs were first diagnosed in the peregrine. *This page:* With a wingspan that can reach 12 feet, the Andean condor is one of the largest flying birds in the world. The bird lives primarily in mountains from 8,000 to 16,000 feet above sea level. *Right:* The last 29 California condors are housed at the San Diego Wild Animal Park and Los Angeles Zoo, while researchers try to determine the birds' habitat need for an eventual return to the wild.

Only those populations of the greater prairie chicken in the central United States persist in any numbers. The last of the eastern population, known as the Heath Hen, died in 1932 on Martha's Vineyard, Massachusetts. *Opposite:* A few scattered sanctuaries are the last hope for the Japanese crane, which requires a large amount of space for successful breeding and has been unable to adapt to concentration and reduction of its territory. The fact that both the Japanese crane and its eggs are considered delicacies by local residents has not helped it.

Once DDT had been removed from the environment, the brown pelican came back in such numbers that it could be removed from the endangered species list.

Habitat preservation is a growing trend. Strict actions against illegal trade are gaining wider support. Limited breeding populations of selected species are being maintained at zoos, on preserves and elsewhere. Indigenous peoples are being helped to realize the value of the animals that inhabit their regions through education programs and tourism-employment opportunities.

Admittedly, it's too late for the 400-plus species and sub-species that man has wiped from the face of the earth over the past 400 years. It's even too late for many of the 10 million species that still inhabit the planet. Some projections foresee a loss of 20 percent of all species by the year 2000.

But many can still be saved. More today than tomorrow.

Once thought to be extinct, more than 1,500 Guadalupe fur seals inhabit the island off Baja California today. *Opposite:* The desire for the sea otter's valuable fur led to the near extinction of the animal by 1911. Protection and a series of reintroductions are helping the animal to recover.

Opposite: The humpback whale is unbelievably agile for its size, often leaping completely clear of the water to fall back head-first. Humpback whales regularly migrate from the summer feeding grounds in the polar region to breeding lagoons thousands of miles south in the tropics. *This page:* The world population of humpback whales is estimated to be fewer than 7,000, although it is slowly increasing. *Overleaf:* The existing population of the gray whale is estimated to be about 16,000. Disturbance from tourists in its breeding lagoons poses a threat to the huge creature.

The blue whale is the largest living animal. It can grow to more than 100 feet in length and weight nearly 200 tons. At birth it is about 23 feet long. *Opposite:* Before man began commercial whaling, there may have been as many as 200,000 blue whales. Today there may be fewer than 7,000.

Index of photography